Winning Isn't Everything (Wait, what?)

Andrews McMeel Publishing
a division of Andrews McMeel Universal
1130 Walnut Street, Kansas City, Missouri 64106

21 22 23 24 25 SDB 10 9 8 7 6 5 4 3 2 1

ISBN: 978-1-5248-7116-1

Library of Congress Control Number: 2021937837

www.andrewsmcmeel.com

Winning Isn't Everything (Wait, what?)

An *In the Bleachers* Collection

Ben Zaehringer

Andrews McMeel
PUBLISHING®

"No, I've never managed to pick one off. I just like seeing their faces when they run by."

“The bullpen’s empty, so I’m just hitting him with the shock collar until he throws strikes.”

“Watch out — this guy might put some spin on the ball.”

“Jeez, Harry! I didn’t mean go *that* long.”

IT LOOKS LIKE KANE IS ABOUT TO CROSS THE FINISH LINE, AND— NO! ALIEN WINS!
FINISH
MOORE + Benz

“This app tells me how many steps I haven’t taken today.”

“Where’s the flag?! He’s clearly constricting the passer!”

“Dewey! Get your head in the game.”

“Hand me my Black & Decker.”

“Nice head fake.”

“Must’ve been a flagrant foul.”

"There's no *way* those buns are real.
He's juicing for sure."

Calisthenics in Hell.

"Good defense, kid!"

"Hey, hey, hey! I said nothin' below the belt!"

"Almost lined up ..."

“Hey! This is a one-on-one tourney. No cellular mitosis.”

uToob
Loading...
How To Pole Vault

"You blew your frontal cortex, but don't worry. We're gonna tape you up and get you back in the game."

TRIATHLON
LEG
2

Gym rats.

"Coach wants a lefty."

"Swearengen, what are you doing?! This is an exhibition game."

“Let’s see that play again in really-really-really-really slow-motion.”

Leroy was later stripped of his medal after testing postive for flotation-enhancing drugs.

“Steroids! Get your steroids!”

"Don't fall for it, Dewey ... They probably put that cap there to psych you out."

Fishing for compliments.

“Looks like they’re going for a walk.”

"Shut that stupid bird up! Squawk!!! Shut that stupid bird up!"

“Now *this* just seems too good to be true.”

“And ... fight!”

"Steroids for sure."

“Don’t foul that guy.”

King Midas on the gridiron.

"This isn't a fair tipoff! When's the last time you clipped your nails?!"

Drama at the Puppy Bowl.

Way-too-personal trainer.

THERE ARE 3 RECEIVERS IN YOUR AREA.
Qber

"Check out this friend request ... Do you know someone named 'Totally100%ARealDeer?'"

START

Dan is disqualified at the weigh-in after testing positive for helium.

“Sorry, we should have told you ... Don’t dribble.”

R.I.P.
TOTAL STEPS:
216,262,501

“Hey, at least you looked cool!”

THE PLAY IS UNDER REVIEW WHILE THE OFFICIALS CONSULT THE TWITTER MOB.
#@!

"Told ya to buy the small tees."

“I’m telling you, man ... These self-riding horses are gonna put us out of business.”

“They gotta turn up the A/C in here.”

"We need a new ball! This one's busted."

"We're out of timeouts ... I'll give you a hundred bucks if you pull the fire alarm."

“What’s the score in L.A.? I’ve been watching the Dallas game.”

Defensive lineman.

"Watch out ... This could get ugly."

“Finally!”

Wrong sport.

“Well, Irv? Was it worth it to wade in there and get your ball back?”

ON YOUR MARK...
START
GET SET...
START

START
LUCKY.
666
667
671

"Go on, girl! Flush 'im out!"

LEMMING RUN
ZERO-K
START
ON YOUR MARK...

"Burt, look! Playoff tickets!"

"Don't worry, I'm just here for your knees."

AH...
AH...
START
ON YOUR MARK...
GET SET...

"They just taste better at the ballpark."

**“It’s not what you’re thinking ...
I left my stick at home.”**

"And remember: nothing below the endoplasmic reticulum."

“If your arms can’t reach, just eat him.”

"*Never* argue with the ump ... Even if the Beatles *are* better than the Stones."

FINISH

"Cheater!"

"Carl, no! Just say 'Mine!' You don't have to mark it."

“If he tries to steal second, eat him.”

"I can see the appeal!"

"Have you noticed we haven't gotten a runner past first this whole game?"

“Someone else should take Bailey’s free throws.”

"Jeez Louise ... *Another* home run?"

“I’ve been watching sports
inside for too long.”

Yes, We're
OPEN

The future of sports.

“Hairball! Ten-yard penalty!”

The stadium experience at home.

“The worst part is, we don’t get our T-shirts until we finish.”

"Lola ... Don't swim in that lane."

MILE
25

"Let's skip this hole."

“Personal foul! Vaporizing the receiver. First down.”

“Wrong way!”

HOT
YOGA

"I found it hovering around the stadium! Can we keep it?! Pleeeeeease?!"

"There may be a spy among us."

“Well, *someone* owes me for seventy-five extra-large pizzas.”

"False start! Number 23. Simon didn't say."

“Why do *I* always have to block?”

"Sorry ... We just sold out."

"Let's work on your grip."

“Told you they work.”

"Someone's coming! We're saved!"

“Morton ... Stop inflating.”

“It’s a photo finish!”

POINT
GUARD DOG
ON DUTY

“Ooh! Double IPA!”

"I dunno ... There's probably a catch."

RIP
Chicken of the

"You have five minutes to finish your tests — and, Dewey, quit calling for a timeout."

“Garrett! Snack *after* the game!”

"No fair!"

“Thag ... Don’t be fool. Take penalty.”

The invention of catch.

“Cool it with the pompoms.”

“Nice spike!”

"To dunk or not to dunk?"

"Psst ... You got this, kid.
I tied his laces together."